7 Principles for Financial Success

Sharing with you the 7 God-given, time-tested principles for succeeding with your personal finances. Giving you the what, why, and the how for winning with your money.

By José R. Figueroa
Personal Finance Coach & Blogger @ Figueroa Financial

Dedication

To my best friend, biggest fan, and the love of my life, my wife *Stacey* for her unwavering support in creating this book. I love you more every day!!!

Contents

Chapter 1
Introduction

"The law of the Lord is perfect, restoring the soul; the testimony of the Lord is sure, making wise the simple."
Psalm 19:7 (NASB)

Why am I writing this book? After all, there are so many books on personal finance available already. Why take the time?

The reason is simple. Our family has been on a financial transformation journey for a little over *7 years* now and I have had some time to reflect on how far we have come. We have experienced the rewards of applying *God-given, time-tested principles* for winning with our personal finances.

Because of the blessings we have received, I wanted to share these <u>*7 Principles for Financial Success*</u> with you. I want you and your family to prosper and be blessed.

Our Story

Here is a picture of our household's financial situation **7** years ago:

- I had a very good, stable job, with great income. But… we were living paycheck to paycheck – u sing credit cards to *make up the difference* every month.
- We had almost **$50K** in unsecured debt (car note, credit cards, student loan, etc.).
- We had *no plan to pay for college* for our son except to consider student loans.
- We had **no savings** for emergencies.
- We had *very little in retirement* funding and no structured plan for savings.
- My wife and I we were *not working together* as a couple.
- We realized *we were not honoring God* in the handling of our finances.

I realized that we needed help. In the fall of 2005, our church offered a financial class (Dave Ramsey's Financial Peace University, FPU) and I attended the (at that time) **13-week** course. As I shared with my wife what I was learning, we started to apply *biblical principles* for sound financial management. We began a *life transforming* journey for our family.

I can thankfully share the positive impact of that decision to get help 7 years ago. Here is where we are today:

- We are *living on a budget*. We have a *plan* for our finances. We have learned to *live on less* than we make.
- We paid off all of our unsecured debt (**$50K**). It took us *29 months*.
- We have a *6* month emergency fund.
- We were able to pay for our son's college *without borrowing money* and without him borrowing money.
- We have a *structured approach* for retirement savings.
- *We are honoring God* with our handling of finances.

My Promise: Help and Hope for Your Finances

I firmly believe that you and anyone can win with personal finances. Sometimes, you just need a little *help* and this I where this book comes in. I want you to have *hope* about your financial situation. I want you and your family to start dreaming again. I don't want anyone left behind in a desperate situation with their finances. There is a way to win with money and it is God's way.

So, over the next few chapters I will un-package what these principles are and you can apply them. In essence, I will give you the what, why, and the how for winning with your finances.

Before we go any further here are the *7 Principles for Financial Success*:

1. Live on less than you make: Get on a Budget.
2. Be prepared: Save for Emergencies.

3. Reduce risk: Avoid consumer debt and payoff the mortgage early.
4. Think about the future: Save for Retirement and save for College.
5. Diversify your investments: Don't put all your eggs in one basket.
6. Love your family well: Work with your spouse. Get insurance. Prepare a will.
7. Give extravagantly.

Are you ready to get started? Let's get going!

"If you do the things you need to do when you need to do them, then someday you can do the things you want to do when you want to do them."
Zig Ziglar

Chapter 2
Principle 1: Live on less than you make.
Get on a Budget.

[28] For which one of you, when he wants to build a tower, does not first sit down and calculate the cost to see if he has enough to complete it?
[29] Otherwise, when he has laid a foundation and is not able to finish, all who observe it begin to ridicule him,
[30] saying, 'This man began to build and was not able to finish.'
Luke 14:28-30 (NASB)

Something you should know about me is that I am huge sports fan. Growing up on the island of Puerto Rico in the 70s and 80s baseball was and it is still my first love. After I moved to the U.S. in 1991, I started following the NBA (Pro Basketball) and the NFL (Pro Football) a lot more closely. Suffice it to say, following sports teams, reading about them, and discussing them with friends (or yelling at the TV) has been a big part of my life.

One common thread I have observed over the years is that regardless of the sport, teams and athletes will struggle from time to time. They will go on a long slump or losing streak. And another common thread is that usually they find their way out of the problem by a simple approach: getting back to basics. You see, most athletes and teams *know what to do*. They understand the mechanics of the game, what each position requires. What happens sometimes is that the information they have in their heads does not translate into *execution*. So to get out of trouble, they commit to going back to basics.

In winning with personal finances, a similar situation exists. Most people understand the basics of what it takes, but few apply the information with great success. So this chapter is devoted to the most fundamental aspect of managing your finances. Yes, the **dreaded "B" word: the Budget**.

I will promise you this: if you can't control your money via a budget, you can't build savings, you can't pay-off debt, and you can't plan for the future. That's where it all starts. So let's get back to the basics of budgeting.

What is a written Budget?

Basically, a budget:

- is a *blueprint* to help you manage and control your finances
- is a way to objectively and comprehensively *discuss money matters* with your spouse (or accountability partner if you are single)
- is a tool that will help you live on less than you make

In essence, as leadership expert John Maxwell says, *"A budget is people telling their money what to do, instead of wondering where it went."*

Why do I need a Budget?

Budgeting is simple but it takes effort and determination. However, I can promise you it is totally worth it. The door to your financial wellness opens only with a working budget.

When you determine to get on a budget every month here are the blessings you can expect:

- You will finally have a *plan* for your money.
- You will have an *objective way* to discuss money matters with your spouse.
- You will gain *insight* into your spending patterns.
- You will learn to *live on less* than what you make.
- You will get *control* over your money.

How do you prepare a Budget?

- Keep it *simple*. A yellow note pad will suffice if you just do it. Today there are also tools on the Internet such as Mint.com or YNAB. Use the tool *that fits you*, but make sure you use something! For me, a basic Excel spreadsheet has served me well over the last **7** years.
- Prepare it every month *before the month* begins. Every month is slightly different.
- Lay out *all* of your monthly income.
- Lay out *all* of your monthly expenses.
- To quote Dave Ramsey: spend every single dollar "*on paper*" and "*on purpose*". In other words, allocate every single dollar to a spending category. This is what is called a "*zero-based*" budget. In the end:

Income – Expenses = Zero

Important Reminders

- Do it *every month*. Plan it and live it. Keep up with your spending.
- Work *with* your spouse (if single, find an accountability partner).
- Use your budget to *gain insight* into your spending patterns.
- Prioritize *giving*.
- Focus on *needs*, not wants.
- Adjust as necessary. It will take you about **90** days to get things under control with your budget. But you will do it!
- Stay with it!!!!

"There is no dignity quite so impressive, and no independence quite so important, as living within your means."
Calvin Coolidge

Chapter 3
Principle 2: Be Prepared. Save for Emergencies.

"There is precious treasure and oil in the dwelling of the wise, But a foolish man swallows it up."
Proverbs 21:20 (NASB)

Growing up on a tropical island, living through tropical storms and hurricanes was part of my way of life. As a matter of fact I distinctly remember hurricane **Eloise** rudely intruding on my 8th birthday in 1975. In Puerto Rico, we always knew the drill: Between June 1st and November 30th we just had to be ready for the potential of lots of rain, loss of power, and interruption to the water service. This meant we had to stock up on non-perishable food items, drinking water, batteries for the radio (to keep up with the news) and flashlights and candles. It also meant making sure you had put enough gas in the cars.

The drill did not change every year because we knew the possibility was very real that we would be hit with a storm. However, it also never failed that people failed to prepare. It was always entertaining (and a little sad) to see the news reports on TV about people rushing to the super market to stock on provisions *the day before* the storm was scheduled to arrive or in some cases *on the day the storm* was scheduled to hit. You would see the anger and desperation of the people as they faced the empty shelves and long lines. I usually thought: Don't you know where you live? Have you not been watching the news? Why is this a surprise and why did you wait until now?

When it comes to our finances, we can become guilty of the same lack of readiness. We know life happens and we will run into some difficulties. I am not trying to be pessimistic, but realistic. Emergency situations will happen to all of us. So, the question is: are you prepared? Most surveys indicate that the majority of Americans don't have **$1,000** in savings to cover an emergency situation. And in spite of some improvement of the last couple of years, American's savings rate still lags considerably compared to other nations. We are saving more than a couple of years ago but not nearly enough.

So what to do about it? The answer is this: you and I need an *emergency fund*.

What's an Emergency Fund?

First let's define what an *"emergency"* situation is with regard to your finances. This would be an unexpected expense outside of your monthly cash flow plan (budget). Some examples include:

- Major Car Repairs
- Home Repairs
- Appliance Replacement
- Uncovered Medical Expense

How much money is needed in an Emergency Fund?

Here is what I would recommend:

- Beginner's emergency fund: **$1,000**
    - **$500** if annual household income is less than **$20K**.
    - Take this step *before* you start paying down on your consumer debt.
    - Most typical "emergencies" can be handled with a beginner's emergency fund. This is what my wife and I had while we got out of debt.

- Full emergency fund: **3 to 6 months** of monthly expenses (based on your monthly budget).
    - Take this step this *after* you pay off your consumer debt.

Why do I need an Emergency Fund?

In one word: peace. My wife and I took the step to become *intentional* about saving money and we can attest to the benefits. Emergencies have become simply inconveniences now that we have an *emergency fund*. If the car breaks down we fix it. If an appliance wears out we replace it.

It took time and sacrifice, but we no longer worry about where the money is coming from or having to decide which credit card has the most available balance. The emergency fund will allow you to absorb the blows that will come from time to time.

> *"He who spends more than he earns is sowing the winds of needless self-indulgence from which he is sure to reap the whirlwinds of trouble and humiliation."*
> *George S. Clason ("The Richest Man in Babylon")*

Chapter 4
Principle 3: Reduce Risk. Avoid Consumer Debt & Pay off the Mortgage early.

"The rich rules over the poor, And the borrower becomes the lender's slave."
Proverbs 22:7 (NASB)

Whether it is credit cards, car loans, or student loans, consumer debt continues to present a major problem to personal finances. Debt is the disease that slowly kills your ability to win with money. It is very hard to prosper with your money when you are weighed down by a big debt burden.

What if all of us took charge of our money? What if we truly learned to live on less than we make? What if you had no payments? What if you had money in the bank? See, debt has been sold to us as tool for prosperity and a way of life. The reality is that debt is simply a modern form of slavery that will keep you from prospering and building wealth.

I believed the lies about debt for a long time. But then, I decided to take control of my finances because that was the only way to prosper. It took time, effort, and sacrifice but it was worth it. So let's talk about why we go into debt, how we can get out of debt, and what rewards can we expect when we learn to live debt-free.

Why do we go into Debt?

If we understand what is at the root of the problem we can address it and change our behavior to match our intellect. Here are the 3 main reasons that cause us to go into debt:

1. *We don't plan for expenses.* Lack of control over our money when we don't have a cash flow plan (i.e., a budget). It seems we don't have enough. Lack of discipline for saving money for major expenses. We mistake a credit line for an emergency fund.

2. ***We seek to take advantage of "deals"***.We spend our time chasing rewards and building up our number of airline miles, points for other purchases, etc.
3. ***We are influenced by the culture.*** We accept that paying interest is a way of life. Interest payments will always keep you from prospering.

Ultimately, we fall victim to the trap of wanting everything now. We exchange the immediate satisfaction of today for the better reward of a stable financial tomorrow.

Why Should I Get Out of Debt?

My wife and I recently celebrated our 5th anniversary of debt-free living. In February of 2008, we finished up paying off all of our consumer debt (credit cards, student loans, car loans, etc.). Life is different for us now and here are *seven real rewards* of debt-free living

1. We don't worry about banks hiking fees or interest rates on credit cards because we don't use credit cards.
2. We don't play the "*Guess Your FICO Score*" game. Don't get me wrong, we do review our credit report on an annual basis to make sure it is accurate. However, we don't rely on the FICO score to tell us we are winning with money so we don't have to jump through all the credit hoops to hit the magic FICO score.
3. We built a 6-month emergency fund. Without the crutch of credit cards we had no alternative. Now, if we have an emergency we have the money to cover it.
4. We have learned contentment with what we have. If we need or want something else, we save and then pay cash for it.
5. We are more selective and patient with our purchases. We just don't buy something just to get miles or points or because we can avoid interest for 90 days.
6. We can save for retirement. We have the money for it since it is not going to monthly debt payments.
7. We are able to give more. We have more disposable income since all the money is not going out to creditors.

I have shared with you the process, the steps for getting out of debt. I have also given you the reasons of why it is a good idea to be debt free.

What I cannot give you is the *desire* and the *passion* to get out of debt. That has to come from you. In order to get out of debt, something has to change in your spirit, in your heart. You will get out of debt when:

- *You admit that using debt will not bring you prosperity*. You basically have to stop believing the lie that debt is a tool to help you win with money. Just look at the high levels of credit card debt, car loan debt, and student loan debt. Ask any of those people to see if they are prospering.
- *You get sick to your stomach when you realize how much interest you are paying*. Do the math exercise on any of the debt items you are carrying today. See how long it is going to take to pay it off by just making the minimum payments. Compute how much that item you bought on credit will cost you in the long run. Just do the math.
- *You get tired of carrying the debt burden*. There has to be a moment when you say: "No more! I am not living this way! I have had it!!!!" Until that happens you will be happy to go along and you will continue to rationalize your debt

How can I get out of Debt?

Taking care of your personal debt is not impossible. But you need to reach a great level of disgust and frustration with yourself. You have to decide that you are done with debt; that you are done being a slave to the lenders; that you are taking control of your financial destiny.

If you are ready to change, if you are truly done borrowing money, there is a way out.

Here are the *6 Steps to Debt Freedom*:

1. Establish a beginner's emergency fund of **$1,000**. You need to have a small cushion so when the car needs a repair you don't have to use a credit card to pay for it.
2. Stop borrowing money. Do not add more debt while you are trying to get out of debt.
3. Stop your retirement contributions *temporarily*. Yes, even if your employer provides a match. You need all the cash flow you can get. Plus you need to focus on getting out of debt instead of having your attention divided on multiple tasks.

4. List all your individual debts (except your mortgage) from *smallest to largest*. Make sure you are current on each one of those debts and keep making the minimum payments. Then start paying extra (as much as you can) on the smallest debt.
5. When you are done paying off that smallest debt, take the amount of that payment and apply it to the next debt on the list.
6. Repeat steps 4-5 until you are done with all of your consumer debt (credit cards, medical bills, car loans, student loans) is paid off. This process is known as the *"Debt Snowball"*.

Here is one more step you need to take: *Pay off* the mortgage early. Imagine getting to your retirement years without a mortgage payment. You don't need a mortgage just because you want to keep a tax deduction. You can achieve the same deduction by increasing your charitable giving.

You could have complete peace of mind knowing that your home is completely yours. Think about it!

"Debt is dumb. Most normal people are just plain broke because they are in debt up to their eyeballs with no hope of help. If you're in debt, then you're a slave because you do not have the freedom to use your money to help change your family tree."
Dave Ramsey

Chapter 5
Principle 4: Think about the Future. Save for Retirement and save for College.

"A good man leaves an inheritance to his children's children, and the wealth of the sinner is stored up for the righteous."
Proverbs 13:22 (NASB)

In this chapter we will turn our attention to the subject of saving money for long term goals. In the previous chapters we focused on getting your finances under control: living on a budget, paying-off consumer debt, having a full emergency fund.

Once you reach a level of stability with your finances you can start thinking about the future. Two of the most critical areas for long term savings are retirement and college expenses. With a solid foundation we can tackle both of them at the same time.

Saving for Retirement

When it comes to retirement savings the conversation might be difficult for you for a number of reasons:

- You might think it's really complicated. I can tell you this: It's really not that complicated.
- You might think it's too late for you, so why bother starting now. Let me remind you that there is no time like today. You still have time.
- You might think that you would like to take your chances with Social Security. Really?

So what I will attempt to do in this section is cover the basics of retirement savings. However, let's get something out of the way first: *it is up to you*.

- It is not the government's responsibility to take care of you after your working days. Even if it was their job, they are completely incapable of doing it right. *It is your job.*
- Your company will not take care of you after your working days. The days of the pension plan after 30 years of service are almost gone. They might provide you with programs to help you plan for retirement, but *it is your job* to take advantage of those opportunities.

When should I start saving for Retirement?

- Ideally, you want to start as soon as possible once you begin working. The sooner the better.
- However, I recommend that you first finish paying off all of your consumer debt (everything but the mortgage) and that you have an emergency fund of **3 to 6** months of expenses in place.

How much should I Save for Retirement?

- You should be saving **15%** of your household income in Roth IRAs and tax-favored retirement plans.
- Tax favored retirement plans include Individual Retirement Arrangements (IRAs), Simplified Employee Pension Plan (SEPP), 401k, 403b, and 457.
- How do I approach funding that 15%?
    1. Fund your 401K or other employer plan up to the match (if applicable). If given the option, choose a Roth 401K plan (because it grows tax free!).
    2. Above the matched amount, fund Roth IRAs. If there is no match provided by your employer start with Roth IRAs.
    3. Complete the 15% of your income by going back to your company's 401K plan.

Important Reminders for Retirement Savings

- Never invest in something you do not understand well enough to explain it to someone else. Seek help from a good investment advisor that is willing to teach you through the process.
- Never take money out of these retirement investments before age **59 1/2**. You'll be hit with high penalties and taxes.
- Never borrow money from your **401k/403B/457**. Any interest you might "pay yourself", will be less than what you would have earned if you left the money alone in a good investment vehicle. Plus, if you lose your job before paying-off the loan, you will have to complete the repayment within **60** days. Otherwise the loan will be considered an early withdrawal subject to taxes and penalties.
- Always roll your **401k/403B/457** balance into a traditional IRA or your Roth IRA if you change jobs.
- Always build wealth slowly. Keep it simple!

Saving for College Expenses

As parents, we are compelled to take care of our kids in every possible way. For most of us, that includes covering the expenses of a college education. Education is critical to success in the market place and typically college graduates tend to have more options for employment.

So the question is not: should you pay for your children's college costs; the question is how to best accomplish that goal without putting your future or the future of your kids in jeopardy. But remember, the college of choice should be commensurate with your household income.

Risks of Borrowing Money for College

The lack of preparation leads us to believe that there is only one way to pay for college: by using debt in the form student loan. Let me share some statistics with you that will help us put the consequences of this belief in perspective:

- The price for room and board at schools has doubled since 1982 and tuition has gone up **439%** in the same period.
- Outstanding college loans now total over **$1 trillion**, an amount that recently exceeded the amount of credit card debt in the US.
- Student loan debt has increased **511%** since 1999. Students now graduate with an average debt of **$25K**, an amount that has grown over **50%** in the past decade.
- More than **45%** of students do not graduate so they are left with the debt and no degree to show for it.
- Since 2008, **85%** of college graduates have been moving back in with parents after they graduate.

In addition to these staggering numbers, there are larger implications of getting deep in student loan debt. This type of debt *cannot be eliminated through bankruptcy*. The decision to go in debt at 18 can follow you for years to come. You know what else happens to you when you have a large amount of student loan debt? You lose career options. You need to stay employed at any job you can get so you can make those payments.

If you think a better option is for you as the parent to take out student loans on behalf of your children, you need to think again. This option simply transfers the debt risk back to you. You might be in a better position to pay the debt back, but the debt could hamper your ability to save for retirement and achieve other financial goals.

Certainly, there has to be a better way than debt and that is through savings. You can pass on to your children the great gift of going through college without debt. It is possible!!!

Options for Saving for College

The best option for college savings is the Education Savings Account (ESA) also known as the "Education IRA".

- You can save up to **$2,000** per year per child and get this: it grows *tax free!!!!*
- Above the ESA, you can use **529** type plans. Focus on those that leave you in control of the funds. Morningstar has done the research on the best and worst of these 529 plans.
- After this, you can move to an **UTMA/UGMA** plan. This stands for **"Uniform Transfer/Gift to Minors Act"**. The account is listed in the child's name and a custodian is named (parent or grandparent). The custodian is the manager of the account until the child turns 21. At age 21 (Age 18 for UGMA), control of the account goes to the child.

Options to Pay for College

- The costs of the school will vary greatly between out-of-state and in-state schools and also between public and private schools, so guide your child to make a wise choice commensurate with what you can afford in your household.
- Starting in a Community College for example will be very cost-effective before the child moves to finish a degree at a 4-year university. At the end of the day employers will look at what the person knows and what they bring to the table more than looking at the university's pedigree.
- In addition, your child can help by making good grades and acing the college entrance exams. That would help with getting scholarships. There are many of those available, so start researching now.
- Having the child work through college is also an option. Our son worked part time all the way through finishing school, so he was part of the process and we reached our goal of a debt-free education for him. And, he graduated on time and with good grades!

You have to start saving now so you can prepare for the day when you need to cover those college expenses. Already started? Great for you and keep going! Not started yet? Don't delay any longer, the time is now. Start today!!!

"No discipline seems pleasant at the time, but painful. Later on however, it produces a harvest of righteousness and peace for those who have been trained by it."
Hebrews 12:11 (NIV)

Chapter 6
Principle 5: Diversify your Investments. Don't put all your eggs in one basket.

"Divide your portion to seven, or even to eight, for you do not know what misfortune may occur on the earth."
Ecclesiastes 11:2

In the previous chapter, we covered subject of saving for the long term goals of retirement and for college. In order to succeed with these goals, you need a solid investment strategy.

Now, I am not a certified financial planner (CFP) or an investment advisor, but I can share how I have approached investing for my future. We have already taken care of college for our son, so our focus is on saving for retirement.

I am keeping my *investing strategy simple*. In both my 401K and Roth IRA I am investing solely in 4 kinds of *Stock Mutual Funds* with a long track record (of at least 10 years). A mutual fund is an investment where thousands of people combine their money to purchase a wide diversity of stocks, bonds or other types of investments. The mutual funds are limited to the type of investment shown in their prospectus.

I am avoiding investing single stocks and I am not investing in any bonds funds. My wife also has an IRA and a Roth IRA and we are applying the same approach to those accounts.

How Would I Direct the Investments?

The idea of diversification is to help you manage the risks. The investment market is fluid and some types of investment will do well at times, while others will struggle. If all your money is one single stock or only in one type of investment fund, your risk is too high. Minimize the risk by spreading out the investment.

Here is how my wife and I are directing our savings in our retirement vehicles:

- **25%** in *Growth Funds* (Mid Cap: Companies that have a market capitalization between $2 and $10 billion)
- **25%** in *Growth & Income Funds* (Large Cap: Companies that have a market capitalization of more than $10 billion)
- **25%** *Aggressive Growth Funds* (Small Cap: Companies that generally have a market capitalization of between $300 million and $2 billion)
- **25%** *International Funds* (Companies that are located anywhere outside of its investors' country of residence. In our case, these would companies outside of the U.S.)

Important Reminders

- Learn about mutual funds. Read, evaluate. Ask for advice from a good investment advisor who is willing to teach you and work with you. Don't work with someone who is just trying to make a sale.
- Look for mutual funds with a good track record of **5** years or longer. I do prefer funds with at least **10** years of a track record.
- Look for funds with returns that average at least **12%**. They are out there! As an example, in 2012, the combination of funds in my 401K had a **19.4%** rate of return.
- Avoid investing in single stocks. If you want to invest in your company's stock, it should be no more than **5-10%** of your retirement investment portfolio.
- Invest consistently and with a long term mentality. Once you go in, stay in and don't panic as the market makes adjustments. Remember, this is a marathon and not a sprint race. Be patient!

"Do not put all your eggs in one basket."
Warren Buffet

Chapter 7
Principle 6: Love your family well. Work with your Spouse. Get Insurance. Prepare a Will.

"But if anyone does not provide for his own, and especially for those of his household, he has denied the faith and is worse than an unbeliever."
I Timothy 5:8 (NASB)

One of the great **"guy movies"** of all time is of course *Braveheart*. Towards the end of the movie, *Sir William Wallace* is facing execution. *Princess Isabelle* can't bear the thought of him dying. In one of the great lines of the movie, he tells her: *"Every man dies, not every man really lives."* Sir William Wallace had given his entire life for a noble and just cause. He gave the example of playing above the line and giving it your all.

The best thing you can do to live your life well is to have and demonstrate love for your family. Here are 3 areas in which you can love your family well.

Work with Your Spouse

In order to win with your finances, you need to have a common understanding with your spouse. Regardless of what your income is and how much you may or may not know about finances, *you need to have shared goals and dreams and also shared responsibility* for doing what's required to achieve those goals and dreams.

Be *open and honest* with each other in the area of finances. Talk about your dreams and your goals as well as your fears. Discuss the mistakes you have made with money before. We all have made mistakes with money, but the important thing is to know what we learned from those mistakes.

Discuss what you know and what you don't know about dealing with money. In your conversations talk about how your respective families handled money, because that will have an effect on your view of handling money.

Finally, your language needs to change from *"you"* and *"me"* to *"we"* and from *"yours"* and *"mine"* to *"ours"*. If you don't work together, you will be working against each other. You are building a life together, so surely you can work together on your money.

Get Insurance

What is the role of insurance? In simple terms, insurance is the tool that is designed to protect you and your family against what might happen. When you have the right level of insurance coverage in place, you are ***transferring the risk*** to another entity (an insurance provider) and you ***pay a premium*** for that risk transfer.

If you think about it, insurance works like an umbrella works when it rains. The umbrella does not stop the rain, but it keeps you from getting wet. Likewise, having the proper insurance won't stop an event, but it will help you weather the storm and minimize the impact to your finances. So what types of insurance do you need?

1. ***Home Insurance/Renters Insurance***: Your home is your most valuable asset so you need to ensure it is properly covered. Be sure that you review your policy on a regular basis so the coverage you have stays in step with the value of your home. Another option is to look for a policy that provides "***guaranteed replacement cost***" for your home. This type of coverage is rare these days, but you should still look for it. If you are renting, you also need to have the proper coverage on your assets to cover against the loss due to theft or fire, as an example.
2. ***Auto Insurance***: You should have both liability and collision coverage on your vehicles. Having at least liability coverage is a legal requirement in the U.S.

3. *Health Insurance*: This is one of the most critical areas to have the proper coverage. Medical bills are consistently a leading cause of personal bankruptcy. In order to save on your premiums, you can increase your deductible and/or co-insurance amounts. You should also evaluate if a *Health Savings Account (HSA)* might be a good option for you. The HSA is a tax-sheltered savings account for medical expenses that works with a high deductible insurance policy.

4. *Long Term Disability Insurance*: This is the type of insurance that would replace your income if you were to be disabled from working for an extended period of time. The best deal in this area is when it is offered by your employer at a discounted rate. You need to look for a policy that is designed to replace **65%** of your income.

5. *Identity Theft Insurance*: Identity theft is one of he fastest growing crimes in the U.S. Over 200 million people have had their identities compromised in a data breach since 2005. The best type of identity theft coverage not only monitors for identity theft, but also assigns a counselor/specialist to deal with the restoration services on your behalf. If your identity is stolen, the biggest and most time-consuming problem is dealing with creditors to restore your good name.

6. *Life Insurance*: If you have anyone depending on your income, you need to make sure they will be taken care of in case something happens to you. The recommended coverage amount is *8 to 10 times* your annual income. The preferred option is to have **20 to 30** year Term Life insurance. It is a less expensive option than Cash Value or Universal /Whole Life type of insurance. The industry is very competitive, so if you are healthy you should be able to get great coverage for a great price.

7. *Long Term Care Insurance*: This is the insurance that would pay for the expenses in a retirement home, at an assisted living facility, or for in-home care. These expenses are very high and if not covered could quickly eat through your retirement nest egg. **69%** of people over the age of **65** will require long-term care at some point in their lives. You should put this insurance in place for yourself as soon as you

turn **60** years old. Be sure to include a *cost-of living rider* and that the pay-out period is *"until death"*.

Prepare a Will

If you don't have a will, you are among **50%** of Americans with children who have neglected this important step. So what are some of your reasons for not dealing with this issue?

You might think it is costly (it is not), or complex (it is not), or that simply you don't have anything to leave to anyone so you don't need a will (oh, but you do).

Or you might just not want to think about your own mortality. However, the reality is that we will all face death and the sooner you face that fact, the better off you will be. So here are *3 reasons you should prepare a will*:

1. *Because it puts you in control:* If you die without a will, the state takes over deciding what happens with your property. The state already has too much say in what happens in our private lives. There is no wisdom in leaving the disposition of your assets to the government.
2. *Because it is simple and cost effective:* You don't need a high priced estate lawyer to do this. For most of us it is really a simple process. Personally I used an online service that provided my wife and I with the required state specific forms for our wills. It just took a few hours and less than **$50** and we are able to put our last wishes on paper.
3. *Because it shows love for your family:* Imagine if something were to happen to you. In the midst of the grief and sorrow of losing you, your family also has to deal with the legal ramifications of what to do with your assets. Don't leave a problem behind. Love your family to the end by taking care of your will preparation today.

So, are you ready to love your family well? We live in a country full of opportunity and you can still leave a legacy. But you have to brave. You have to be daring. You have to choose to be above average. Take care of it today!

"Every right implies a responsibility; every opportunity, an obligation; every possession, a duty."
John D. Rockefeller

Chapter 8
Principle 7: Give Extravagantly.

[6] Now this I say, he who sows sparingly will also reap sparingly, and he who sows bountifully will also reap bountifully.
[7] Each one must do just as he has purposed in his heart, not grudgingly or under compulsion, for God loves a cheerful giver.
[8] And God is able to make all grace abound to you, so that always having all sufficiency in everything, you may have an abundance for every good deed;
2 Corinthians 9:6-8 (NASB)

As I wrote in the introduction to this book, I want you to be incredibly successful with your finances. I want to help you create a plan to get control over and win with your money. As an Evangelical Christian, I will always speak, teach and coach on money management from God's point of view as laid out in Scripture.

I firmly believe a good understanding and practice of godly giving stewardship principles is at the core of a successful financial plan. Generosity is a distinguishing trademark of people who prosper with money.

However, from all the giving statistics, stewardship and giving are difficult topics for the people of God. On average only about **25%** of Christians tithe (i.e., give a tenth) of their regular income to their local church. Many churches tend to struggle to make their annual budget, which forces them to cut or limit their programs. How do we improve on that?

The last thing I want to do is book you a reservation for a guilt trip about giving. But I also know that in order for you to win with your finances, you need to incorporate giving on a regular basis. I believe God wants us to manage His money according to His ways. So I want to talk about the subject from God's perspective.

With Him, just like with anything else in our Christian walk, what matters most is the condition of our hearts and not the actions we take. When our hearts are in the right place, the behavior will follow.

Reasons for Giving

If you are asking, "why should I give?" I would like to give you my motivation for giving. These come from my Christian worldview and from my personal experience.

1. ***God is the Owner:*** I understand that I am an asset manager for God and that He owns it all (Psalm 24:1). He does not "need" my money. Plus, I will give an account to Him on the sum of my life, and finances are just a part of the account (2 Corinthians 5:9-10). So giving is really a matter of ***obedience***.
2. ***God is the Provider:*** Everything comes from God. One of the great preachers and Bible teachers of our generation, Dr. David Jeremiah, has put it best: ***"God is a God of grace. His grace provides strength to earn, generosity to give, and humility to receive."*** So giving is really a matter of ***thanksgiving***.
3. ***God is the Example:*** He gave the ultimate gift by giving His Son as the Savior of the whole world (I John 4:9-10). Giving makes us more like God and Christ. They are givers. As we grow into the likeness of Christ, we should grow in the aspect of giving as we seek to be like Him (Romans 8:29). So giving is really a matter of ***spiritual maturity***.

Benefits of Giving

You might also ask, ***"What's in it for me?"*** First, you will get to experience the joy of giving. God is the great Giver and He has given His best to us. When we give, we are simply emulating our Heavenly Father.

Second, when you support the work of your church, you get to participate in the great adventure of doing God's work. When your money is out of control, when you are deeply in debt, it is very difficult to join in advancing God's kingdom.

Finally, when you give to help others, you put love and compassion into action. The purpose of getting your money management under control, the purpose of building wealth, is so you can share the blessings with others. You can only give hope, when you yourself have hope. Trust me, *it is better to give than to receive* (Acts 20:35).

"God is the great giver. The great provider. The fount of every blessing. Absolutely generous and utterly dependable. The resounding and recurring message of Scripture is clear: God owns it all. God shares it all. Trust him, not stuff!"
Max Lucado ("Fearless")

Chapter 9
Conclusion: The Purpose of Wealth

^{17} Teach those who are rich in this world not to be proud and not to trust in their money, which is so unreliable. Their trust should be in God, who richly gives us all we need for our enjoyment.
^{18} Tell them to use their money to do good. They should be rich in good works and generous to those in need, always being ready to share with others.
^{19} By doing this they will be storing up their treasure as a good foundation for the future so that they may experience true life.
I Timothy 6:17-19 (NLT)

As we get to the end of this book, I don't want you to lose sight of the fact that the pursuit of wealth is not just a purpose unto itself. As I look at the Scripture passage above, I wanted to leave you what it teaches me about wealth.

I hope you take these to heart as you continue in your journey towards financial wellness.

1. We should not take pride or put our trust in our wealth. When we do this, we turn our wealth into an idol and it becomes the primary driver of our lives (Matt 6:24).
2. Earthly riches are temporary and can be here today and gone tomorrow. A job loss, an illness, poor decisions, or a dramatic socioeconomic event could really cause our wealth to disappear (Job 1:21-22).
3. Our trust should be in God who is the One who provides everything in our lives. All good things come from Him including our ability to work, earn money, and prosper (Deut 8:18).
4. Live with a heart full of gratitude (I Thess 5:18; Col 3:15).
5. It is good to enjoy the fruits of our labor. There is nothing wrong with spending money wisely (Eccl 5:18-19).
6. Our wealth should be used to do good works and to help those in need. We should always be ready to share from what the Lord has provided for us (Gal 6:10).

7. What we do for others in this life has more eternal value than anything shown on our balance sheet (Matt 6:19-21).

"We are not cisterns made for hoarding, we are channels made for sharing."
Billy Graham

Appendix A. About the Author

José Figueroa was born and raised in Puerto Rico but has been living in the Lone Star State of Texas for over **22** years. After spending time in Houston and Austin, he is now living in Frisco, just north of Dallas. He has a passion for helping people *get control of their money*. José understands from personal experience that managing finances can be challenging and overwhelming.

José married his wife Stacey in March of 2003. They are members of Prestonwood Baptist Church in Plano. They have one grown son (Brent Jett) who works as a Graphic Designer in Austin, TX.

Services Offered via Figueroa Financial

- **Individual/Couples Financial Coaching:** Offering you information and education built on biblical principles for managing finances. Help for getting on a budget, building an emergency reserve, or breaking out of the slavery of consumer debt.
- **Financial Seminars for Churches and Non-Profit Organizations:** Our **4-week financial seminar** is ideal for churches and non-profit organizations. The seminar covers the topics of how to live on a budget, how to save money, and how to get out of debt. The last session brings it all together around the subject of giving and stewardship.
- **Personal Finance Blog:** Weekly blog posts focusing on how to improve your money management skills.

Contact Information: You can reach José via any of the following methods:

- Website: www.figueroafinancial.com
- e-mail: jose.figueroa310@gmail.com

Connect Via Social Media

Facebook: www.facebook.com/figueroafinancial

Twitter: https://twitter.com/FigueroaFin

LinkedIn: http://www.linkedin.com/in/jrfigueroa

Google+:
https://plus.google.com/u/0/b/111459341392513036380/111459341
392513036380/posts

Pinterest: http://pinterest.com/jfigueroa310/financial-coaching/

www.ingramcontent.com/pod-product-compliance
Lightning Source LLC
Chambersburg PA
CBHW071551170526
45166CB00004B/1626